I can't figure out why we haven't had a book like this before, but it's just what we need. Allberry has written the perfect book to hand to skeptics and wobbly believers. The tone is irenic, the content firm, and the length manageable. He covers the necessary texts and answers—in an intelligent, yet brief and winsome way—the most common questions and objections. I will be recommending this book often in the years ahead. **Kevin DeYoung,**
Pastor, author and Gospel Coalition blogger

Empathetic and wise, learned and clear, hopeful and kind—this book by Sam Allberry is on a topic that can be very challenging. It would be helpful for just about anyone to read.
Mark Dever, Pastor, Capitol Hill Baptist Church

This is an excellent book. It is real and sensitive, bold and biblical. It pulls no punches but is never strident or angular. Sam is clearly writing from the heart, and with a heart for Christ, his people and the world. **Steve Timmis, Executive Director, Acts 29**

This is a very important book containing so much gospel wisdom.
Al Mohler,
President, The Southern Baptist Theological Seminary

The gospel is good news, for homosexuals too. The gospel doesn't define us by our temptations but by the righteousness of Christ. This book sets forth the biblical case. The author captures perfectly the gospel's call to repentance and offer of mercy. Read this book and consider how God is calling you to love, in word and in deed, all of those around you. **Russell D. Moore, President,**
Ethics and Religious Liberty Commission,
Southern Baptist Convention

Sam writes with genuine pastoral warmth out of his own personal experience. He argues convincingly that, far from being anti-gay, God loves those who experience same-sex attraction and that the gospel is good news for us too. **Jonathan Berry, Director, True Freedom Trust**

Is God Anti-gay? is truly marvellous. Sam's humanity shines through every page; his understanding of weakness undergirds the whole; his compassion for those facing that which he himself faces each day is deeply moving. This book would make an excellent resource for pastors and elders to keep on hand, given that this is an issue which is set to become more, not less, significant and contentious.
**Carl R. Trueman,
Professor of Historical Theology & Church History,
Westminster Theological Seminary**

EXCELLENT! Short, clear, kind, understanding... this needs to be widely distributed. **Jonathan Leeman, Editorial Director, 9Marks, blogger and author**

This short book is outstanding. Sam Allberry handles people carefully, texts wisely, and issues sensitively, and the result is a supremely helpful book on perhaps the most challenging issue western Christians face today. I highly recommend it. **Andrew Wilson, pastor and blogger at thinktheology.co.uk**

Every minister should read this book and we should endeavor to get it into the hands of as many of our congregation as possible.
Paul Levy, Reformation 21 blog

Is God anti-gay?

And other questions about homosexuality,
the Bible and same-sex attraction

Sam Allberry

Questions
Christians ask

Is God anti-gay? (Revised and Expanded Edition)
And other questions about homosexuality, the Bible and same-sex attraction
Part of the *Questions Christians Ask* series
© Sam Allberry/The Good Book Company, 2015.
Reprinted 2015, 2016, 2017 (twice), 2018.

Published by
The Good Book Company
Tel (North America): (1) 866 244 2165
Tel (UK): 0333 123 0880
International: +44 (0) 208 942 0880
Email (North America): info@thegoodbook.com
Email (UK): info@thegoodbook.co.uk

Websites
North America: www.thegoodbook.com
UK & Europe: www.thegoodbook.co.uk
Australia: www.thegoodbook.com.au
New Zealand: www.thegoodbook.co.nz

ISBN: 9781908762313 | Printed in the UK

Design by André Parker

Contents

Introduction

first began to properly understand something of my sexuality around the same time that I began to understand Jesus Christ.

I was in my final weeks of high school. Exams were coming to an end and we were all looking forward to the prospect of a long, study-free summer. It had been a hectic final few months. A couple of uncomfortable home truths were sinking in. The first was that it is quite hard to prepare for exams when you haven't paid much attention in class. Revising is much harder when you haven't done much "vising."

The other home truth was even more uncomfortable. I had always been someone who formed close friendships, but I was now beginning to realize there was something a bit more than that going on. Though I'd had a couple of girlfriends, I'd never felt the same kind of bond as I had with one or two of my close male friends. As the long summer began and there was less going on to distract me, the truth began to bite. The words began to form in my mind: *I think I'm gay.*

This was not a welcome development. I wanted to be like everyone else, and to be into what everyone else was into. I wanted to have feelings for girls like my friends had. And yet, instead of having feelings for girls *with* my friends, I was finding myself having feelings *for* my friends.

It was during this same period that I got to know some Christians for the first time. I was working Saturday afternoons in a local Christian-run coffee shop, and this was the first time I'd ever really got to know Christians my own age. They became fast friends and when, after exams were over and I had nothing else to do, they invited me to their church youth group, I decided to go along. I liked these guys and was interested to know more about what they believed. The message of Jesus, it turned out, was quite different from what I had imagined...

The message I heard

When Jesus began his public ministry, he made the following announcement, and it takes us right to the heart of his message:

> After John was put in prison, Jesus went into Galilee, proclaiming the good news of God. "The time has come," he said. "The kingdom of God has come near. Repent and believe the good news!"
>
> *Mark 1 v 14-15*

Jesus says the kingdom of God has come near. Whatever God had planned to do to put right the wrongs of this world, *right then* was when he was doing it. It was all about to kick off.

And the response Jesus looks for is **repentance** and **faith**.

Repentance means turning around, to change course. The implication is pretty clear and a little uncomfortable: *we're not heading in the right direction*. We're like the elderly man I read about recently in our local newspaper: in a moment of confusion in the middle of the night, he'd ended up driving a mile or so on the wrong side of the motorway. Thankfully at that hour there was hardly anything coming the other way; if it had happened when the commuters were up, it would have been a very different story.

Jesus says that we're heading in the wrong direction, and that the rush hour of God's purposes is heading toward us. We need to change direction and line up with what God is doing. And that means **believing the gospel**: the announcement that, through Jesus' death and resurrection, we can be put right with God; that we are being offered a fresh start to begin to live as God always meant us to. This is his message.

And it's his message for all people. When Jesus burst onto the scene, he didn't subdivide humanity into categories and give each one a separate message. One for the introverts; another for the extroverts. One (with logical charts and bullet points) for left-brain types, and one (with different colors and ambient music) for the right-brain folk.

God's message for gay people is the same as his message for everyone. *Repent and believe.* It is the same invitation to find fullness of life in God, the same offer of forgiveness and deep, wonderful, life-changing love.

Same-sex attraction vs "gay"

It was this message I first heard at my friends' church, the message I have tried to live in the light of in the years since. Through it all, as someone who lives with homosexuality, I have found biblical Christianity to be a wonderful source of comfort and joy. God's word to me on this issue at times feels confusing and difficult. But it is nevertheless deeply and profoundly good. The gospel of Jesus is wonderful news for someone who experiences same-sex attraction.

I used the term "same-sex attraction" just then because an immediate challenge is how I describe myself. In western culture today the obvious term for someone with homosexual feelings is "gay." But in my experience this often refers to far more than someone's sexual orientation. It has come to describe an identity and a lifestyle.

When someone says they're gay, or for that matter, lesbian or bisexual, they normally mean that, as well as being attracted to someone of the same gender, their sexual preference is one of the fundamental ways in which they see themselves. And it's for this reason that I tend to avoid using the term. It sounds clunky to describe myself as "someone who experiences same-sex attraction." But describing myself like this is a way for me to recognize that the kind of sexual attractions I experience are not fundamental to my identity. They are part of *what I feel* but are not *who I am* in a fundamental sense. I am far more than my sexuality.

Take another kind of appetite. I love meat. A plate without a slab of animal on it just doesn't feel right to me. But my love for meat does not mean I would want someone to think that "carnivore" was the primary category through which to understand me. It is part of the picture, but does not get to the heart of who I am. So I prefer to talk in terms of being someone who experiences homosexual feelings, or same-sex attraction (SSA for short in what follows).

And as someone in this situation, what Jesus calls me to do is exactly what he calls anyone to do. Take another well-known saying of Jesus:

> Then he called the crowd to him along with his disciples and said: "Whoever wants to be my disciple must deny themselves and take up their cross and follow me."　　　　　　　　　*Mark 8 v 34*

It is the same for us all—"whoever." I am to deny myself, take up my cross and follow him. Every Christian is called to costly sacrifice. Denying yourself does not mean tweaking your behavior here and there. It is saying *"no"* to your deepest sense of who you are, for the sake of Christ. To take up a cross is to declare your life (as you have known it) forfeit. It is laying down your life for the very reason that your life, it turns out, is not yours at all. It belongs to Jesus. He made it. And through his death he has bought it.

Ever since I have been open about my own experiences of homosexuality, a number of Christians have said something like this: "The gospel must be harder for you than it is for me," as though I have more to give up than they do. But the fact is that the gospel demands *everything* of *all of us*. If someone thinks the gospel has somehow slotted into their life quite easily, without causing any major adjustments to their lifestyle or aspirations, it is likely that they have not really started following Jesus at all.

And just as the cost is the same for all of us, so too are the blessings. Over the past few years of wrestling with this issue, this has become one of my favorite sayings of Jesus:

> Come to me, all who are weary and burdened, and
> I will give you rest.   *Matthew 11 v 28*

This is a wonderful promise. Jesus assumes that, left to ourselves, we are weighed down. Life out of sync with God does that to us. But as we come to Jesus we find rest. Not just rest in the sense of a lazy weekend afternoon or a long sleep-in on a day off. Jesus means something far deeper: rest in the sense of things with God being the way they're meant to be. Rest in the sense of living along the grain of who we really are and how God wants us to live. Rest in the sense of being able truly to flourish as the people God made us to be.

Is God anti-gay? *No.*

But he is against who all of us are by nature, as those living apart from him and for ourselves. He's anti *that* guy, whatever that guy looks like in each of our lives. But because he is bigger than us, better than us, and able to do these things in ways we would struggle to, God loves that guy too. Loves him enough to carry his burden, take his place, clean him up, make him whole, and unite him forever to himself.

Being a Christian and living as a Christian with SSA raises all sorts of questions—questions I hope we can cover in this book. My own experiences of homosexuality do not mean that I can speak for everyone for whom this is an issue. Over the years I have got to know many people for whom this is not an abstract issue. Men and women; young and old; some with a faith; and some who are hostile to Christianity; those who have shared with me in strictest confidence; and those who publicly and proudly self-identify as gay. Every one of those conversations has been a privilege. Some have shared stories of painful rejection (in one case, of being spat at by his peers); others of surprised acceptance. In some cases there have been strong similarities with my own experiences and feelings, and in other cases it has been very different. So I am not presuming to speak for others. My aim instead is to try to take each question and to see what the Bible has to say.

Almost the first to be asked is: "What does the Bible actually say about homosexuality?" and we'll get to that soon. But the more I look at the Bible, the more convinced I am that what it says about sexuality makes most sense in light of what it says in general about sex and marriage.

So that's where we'll begin…

Chapter 1

Homosexuality and God's design

Many people have the idea that the Bible is somehow disapproving of sex, as though it was something we discovered behind God's back and without his complete approval. But Genesis shows us something very different.

God is the one who made humankind male and female, and God is the one who commanded them to "be fruitful and increase in number" (Genesis 1 v 28). Sex is God's idea. It was not our invention but his gift. And it was not begrudgingly given, as if God said: "Well go on, if you *have* to." No, God gave us a means of reproduction that was not just functional but deeply pleasurable. Sex is a sign of his goodness.

Genesis 1 and 2 show us the two purposes of sex. These chapters provide two complementary accounts of creation. The first (in Genesis 1) is like a wide-angle lens, describing the creation of the physical world and all life within it. The second (in Genesis 2) zooms in on the creation of the first man and woman.

In Genesis 1, humanity is created in God's image and tasked with ruling the earth and its creatures. In this context, the point of the sexual difference between man and woman is reproduction. Increasing in number will enable them to fill the earth and be present everywhere to rule over it.

But in Genesis 2 the differences between the sexes are presented in a different light. Adam is created first, and yet it is "not good" for him to be alone. By himself he is unable to fulfill the purposes for which God created him. The remedy to this is the creation of the first woman. In contrast to the various animals Adam has just named, the woman perfectly corresponds to him:

The man said,
> "This is now bone of my bones
> and flesh of my flesh;
she shall be called "woman,"
> for she was taken out of man.

Genesis 2 v 23

She is like him in the right way (*made of the same stuff*) and unlike him in the right way (*woman, rather than man*). She is a different example of the same kind of thing as him—she shares his nature, his vocation, and his very life. It is this *complementarity* that leads to profound unity between them when they eventually come together in sexual union:

> That is why a man leaves his father and mother and is united to his wife, and they become one flesh.
> *Genesis 2 v 24*

The purpose of sex here is to express and deepen the unity between them.

And the writer makes it clear that he is no longer just talking about Adam and Eve. We're not being told about this first human couple on the off-chance we're interested in our ancient family history. No, their story is true for all of humankind. It sets up a pattern that we see repeated in every generation. The writer pulls back from their immediate setting to make the general observation: "That is why a man leaves his father and mother and is united to his wife..."

What was going on with Adam and Eve explains what has gone on ever since. The perfect "fit" between the two of them is the foundation for every human marriage since. The account is not just about their union but every marriage union.

The man and woman become "one flesh." Thanks to a few too many love songs, this kind of language—of "two becoming one"—may sound a little clichéd to our ears. But it's not just describing the sense of togetherness a couple might feel while caught up in the height of passion. It is something objective and real. Jesus teaches that it is God who joins couples together in marriage and makes them one (Matthew 19 v 6). God himself produces this union between them. Physically, psychologically, emotionally and spiritually, two people are becoming knitted together. God has designed it to work that way.

And it works very well. The binding effect of sex in a relationship is what makes the breakdown of a sexual relationship so profoundly painful. It's not what we're designed for. And the more that union is forged and then broken, the more our capacity for deep and abiding unity is diminished.

Sexuality is a little like a post-it note. The first time you use it, it sticks well. But when it is reapplied too many times, it loses its capacity to stick to anything. We are simply not designed for multiple sexual relationships. Sex becomes less relational, more functional and less satisfying as a result. Casual sexual encounters are made to look harmless and fun in most sitcoms, but the consequences in real life are far more serious—emptiness, brokenness and devastation. We should not be surprised: sex is designed to irreversibly bind two people together.

So Genesis 1 – 2 shows us that God is *for* sex. It also shows us that sex is for marriage.

How does marriage fit in with this?

In his own teaching Jesus reinforces the sexual ethics of Genesis 1 – 2. He characterizes all sexual activity outside of marriage as evil:

> What comes out of a person is what defiles them. For it is from within, out of a person's heart, that

evil thoughts come—sexual immorality, theft, murder, adultery, greed, malice, deceit, lewdness, envy, slander, arrogance and folly. All these evils come from inside and defile a person.

Mark 7 v 20-23

The term we translate as "sexual immorality" is the Greek word *porneia*, an umbrella term for all sexual activity outside marriage. Such behavior Jesus describes as evil and defiling.

Elsewhere, Jesus reinforces the permanence and exclusivity of marriage:

Some Pharisees came to him to test him. They asked, "Is it lawful for a man to divorce his wife for any and every reason?" "Haven't you read," he replied, "that at the beginning the Creator 'made them male and female,' and said, 'For this reason a man will leave his father and mother and be united to his wife, and the two will become one flesh'? So they are no longer two, but one flesh. Therefore what God has joined together, let no one separate."

Matthew 19 v 3-6

Jesus underlines what we have already seen in Genesis. We are created male and female. Humanity is gendered. We are not just human beings, but men and women. And this has been the case from "the beginning." Twas ever thus. Yes, gender is something we humans interpret and lend cultural expression to, but it is not something that we invent or fully define. It is how God created us.

Next, Jesus shows us that this sexual difference is why we have marriage. We are male and female: "For this reason a man will leave..." It is because we are male and female that we have the phenomenon of marriage. Marriage is based on gender. Marriage would not exist without the sexual differences between men and women.

It is this sexual difference that accounts for the depth of union between the man and woman. Eve was created out of Adam: made from his body. Their one-flesh union is therefore something of a re-union, joining together what had originally been one.

These truths help us understand some of the purposes for marriage in the Bible:

1. Human marriage is meant to reflect something of God's nature. In the most famous creed in the Old Testament, believers are reminded that: "The LORD our God, the LORD is one" (Deuteronomy 6 v 4). The particular Hebrew word for "one" (*'ehad*) is not primarily a mathematical observation—that there is one of him, as opposed to two or five. It is an assertion about God's nature. He is One. There is a unity to him. He is of a piece. We see in the Bible that this God is Trinity—he is Father, Son and Holy Spirit. Three different persons. But all that this triune God is, does, and says is perfectly integrated. One.

This very same word is used in Genesis 2 v 24 to describe the union of the man and woman in marriage. They become one (*'ehad*) flesh. Marriage is a wonderful God-given way for humanity to reflect the unity and diversity that is seen in the Trinity. God's oneness is not sameness, as though the three persons of the Trinity were identical to one another. It is unity in difference, not uniformity. And the same is true of the union of a man and a woman. There is this same kind of oneness that comes when male and female are united in this way.

The same is not true of gay sex. Two men or two women cannot become one flesh. They cannot become one (*'ehad*) in the way that God is one and in the way that a man and a woman are one. They can have a union of sorts, but it is not of the kind that is uniquely possible with a heterosexual marriage.

This is not to say that commitment and faithfulness cannot be present in a gay relationship, or that they automatically exist in a heterosexual relationship just by virtue of the couple's heterosexuality. I know gay couples where there is impressive loyalty and commitment, just as I can think of some heterosexual marriages that are floundering and failing at this very point. The issue is not the feelings of commitment that two people may have for one another, but rather, the kind of union God gives to a man and woman when they become physically one. It is this complementarity that is fundamental to marriage. However else we may differ from one another in temperament, personality type, culture and background, it is ultimately the joining of male-female that leads to the one-flesh experience.

2. This one-flesh union is designed to be the way in which Adam and Eve fulfill God's com-

mand to "be fruitful and multiply and fill the earth" (Genesis 1 v 28, ESV). From this union flows the possibility of new life—for children to result from it. This is reflected in the Old Testament book of Malachi: "Did [the LORD] not make them one, with a portion of the Spirit in their union? And what was the one God seeking? Godly offspring." (Malachi 2 v 15, ESV). Procreation is not the sole purpose of marriage (those unable to have children are no less married because of that), but it is clear that procreation is intended to be rooted in marriage.

3. Human marriage is not just meant to reflect something of God's nature. **It is also meant to reflect the grace that God shows to his people in Christ:**

> "For this reason a man will leave his father and mother and be united to his wife, and the two will become one flesh." This is a profound mystery— but I am talking about Christ and the church.
> *Ephesians 5 v 31-32*

Paul is saying that marriage is about the relationship Jesus has with the church. It, too, is a union between two different yet complementary entities. The church is not the same as Christ, and Christ is not the same as the church (a wonderful truth given the imperfections of the church!). And it is because Christ is different to his people that he is able to draw them to himself, pledge himself to them, and have them be united to him. Human marriage is a reflection of this supreme, heavenly marriage between Christ and his people. It is one of the reasons why Christians are resistant to allowing marriage to be defined in such as way as to include gay couples. A man and a man, or a woman and a woman, cannot reflect the union of Christ and the church; instead these only reflect Christ and Christ, or church and church.

The Bible's teaching on sex and marriage is the foundation for how Christians are to think about the whole issue of sexuality today. The teaching of Genesis, reinforced and expanded by Jesus in his own ministry, is that sex is a good gift that God has given exclusively for marriage, and that in order for marriage to fulfill the purposes for which God instituted it, marriage must be between one man and one woman.

All of which raises a huge and urgent question: *where does homosexuality fit into all this?*

Chapter 2

Homosexuality and the Bible

It is a surprise to many people to discover that there are only a handful of passages in the Bible that directly mention homosexuality. It's just not an issue that comes up much. Where it does, however, the Bible has important and clear things to say about homosexuality. So it won't do to say that this teaching, because of its relative infrequency, does not matter. The Bible does not frequently make direct reference to how we are to care for creation, but that does not let us off the hook from following what is said in the places where it does.

But at the very least, this does show us that the Bible is not *fixated* on homosexuality. It is not what the Bible is *about*. Our understanding of what the Bible *does* say on the subject therefore needs to be read in the light of the bigger themes of Scripture. What the Bible says about homosexuality does not represent everything

...d wants to say to homosexual people; it is not the whole message of Christianity. And so the passages below need to be looked at as part of the wider message of the gospel—the announcement of what God has done for us in Christ, and the need for repentance and faith.

Christians who want to explain the Christian faith to gay friends need to know that what the Bible says about homosexuality is not the only thing they need to explain, and it is probably not the first thing, or even the main thing, they need to focus on.

The first two passages that directly mention homosexuality come from the Old Testament.

1. Genesis 19

The city of Sodom in Genesis 19 has become so associated with homosexual conduct that its name has for many generations been a pejorative term for gay sex. *But is sodomy really what Sodom is about?*

The account begins with the arrival of two angels at the city gate, charged with determining whether or not the outcry that has reached God about it is justified. The angels appear as men, and are strongly discouraged from spending the night out in the open in the city square—itself a hint as to where things are at in Sodom. They lodge instead with Lot.

It is when the sun sets that things get nasty:

> But before they lay down, the men of the city, the men of Sodom, both young and old, all the people to the last man, surrounded the house. And they called to Lot, "Where are the men who came to

you tonight? Bring them out to us, that we may
know them."   *Genesis 19 v 4-5, ESV*

On its own, this might seem a damning verdict. But
later parts of the Old Testament accuse Sodom of quite
different sins: oppression, adultery, lying, abetting crim-
inals, arrogance, complacency and indifference to the
poor. None of these even *mention* homosexual conduct.
This has led some people to wonder if we have read homosexuality into the Genesis narrative, when in fact the
real issue was social oppression and injustice. But a close
look at the story makes it clear that homosexuality was
in fact involved.

First, although the Hebrew word for "know" (*yada*)
can just mean to "get to know" someone (rather than to
"know" them sexually), it is clear both from the crowd's
aggression, and from Lot's dreadful attempt at offering
them his daughters as an alternative, that they are looking for much more than a quiet chat over a cup of coffee.

Secondly, this crowd is not a small, unrepresentative
group. It is very clear this is the whole male community:
"the men of Sodom, both young and old, all the people
to the last man." This is how the *city* is behaving. This
is what Sodom does.

This explains what happens next; the angels warn
Lot that judgment is imminent (v 13). They have discovered all they need to know. The outcry against Sodom is justified.

In the New Testament, Jude adds an important insight:

In a similar way, Sodom and Gomorrah and the surrounding towns gave themselves up to sexual immorality and perversion. They serve as an example of those who suffer the punishment of eternal fire.

Jude 7

What happened at Sodom is clearly meant to be a cautionary tale. They are an example of facing God's judgment. Peter says much the same: Sodom and Gomorrah stand as "an example of what is going to happen to the ungodly" (2 Peter 2 v 6). And Jude makes it clear that their ungodliness involved sexual immorality. They were punished for sexual sin along with the other sins of which they were guilty. Their destruction serves as a warning: *God takes sexual sin very seriously.*

Jude also highlights the perversity of their sexual desires: they pursued "unnatural desire" (ESV); literally, *unnatural flesh.* Some have suggested that this relates to the fact that the visitors to the city were angelic; both Jude and Peter also reference angelic sin earlier in their letters. But these angels appeared *as men*, and the baying crowd outside Lot's house showed no evidence of knowing they were angelic. Their desire was to have sex with the *men* staying with Lot.

So it was not only the violent way in which the crowd were attempting to satisfy their sexual cravings that was ungodly, but also the nature of the cravings as well. A parallel episode in Judges 19 indicates it is not just pagan Sodom, but also the people of God who commit this kind of sin.

2. Leviticus 18 and 20

Leviticus contains two prohibitions against homosexual activity:

> You shall not lie with a male as with a woman; it is an abomination.   *Leviticus 18 v 22, ESV*

> If a man lies with a male as with a woman, both of them have committed an abomination; they shall surely be put to death; their blood is upon them.
> *Leviticus 20 v 13, ESV*

"An abomination" is often used to describe idolatry, and so some suggest these verses are not prohibiting homosexual behavior in general, but only the cultic prostitution associated with pagan temples. But the language used is not that specific; the passages refer in general to a man lying with a man "as with a woman," without specifying a particular context for that act. Moreover, the surrounding verses in both Leviticus 18 and 20 forbid other forms of sexual sin that are general in nature, such as incest, adultery and bestiality.

None of these have any connection with pagan temples or idolatry. These things are morally wrong, irrespective of who is doing them and where they are happening. It is also important to see that the second of these two verses (Leviticus 20 v 13) prohibits both male parties equally. We can't write it off as only prohibiting things like gay rape or a forced relationship. Leviticus prohibits even general, consensual homosexual activity.

It is also important to see that homosexual behavior is not the *only* sin to be described as "an abomination" in the Bible. Leviticus refers to other sexual sins in exactly the same way, and Proverbs lists deceitful speech, pride and murder as equally abominable to God. Homosexual sin is not in a category of its own in this regard.

3. Romans 1 v 18-32

Romans 1 has a lot to say about the nature and character of homosexual behavior. It's worth reading the whole chapter before you read on...

Paul's aim in these early chapters is to demonstrate that the whole world is unrighteous in God's sight and therefore in need of salvation. In Romans 1 v 18-32 he homes in on the pagan Gentile world, describing its turning from God and embracing of idolatry and wickedness. The particular details in the passage may indicate that Paul is using the Greco-Roman culture surrounding his readers as a case in point.

Gentile society faces God's wrath because it has suppressed the truth that God has revealed about himself in creation (verses 18-20). In the verses that follow, Paul illustrates how this has happened, giving three examples of how what has been known about God has been exchanged for something else: they exchange the *glory* of God for images of creatures (v 23); the *truth* of God for a lie, leading to full-blown idolatry, worshiping created things (v 25); and they reject the *knowledge* of God (v 28), exchanging "natural" relations for "unnatural" ones:

> Because of this, God gave them over to shameful
> lusts. Even their women exchanged natural sexual
> relations for unnatural ones. In the same way the
> men also abandoned natural relations with women
> and were inflamed with lust for one another. Men
> committed shameful acts with other men, and
> received in themselves the due penalty for their
> error. *Romans 1 v 26-27*

Two important and sobering truths are apparent from
these verses:

a. Homosexuality is unnatural

Paul describes both lesbian and male homosexual behavior as "unnatural." This is clearly a massive thing for
the Bible to say and, correspondingly, a very hard thing
for many people to hear. Some have wondered whether
"unnatural" might refer to what is natural to the people themselves. If so, Paul would be talking about heterosexual people engaging in homosexual activity and
thereby going against their "natural" orientation. Paul
would therefore not be condemning all homosexual behavior, but only that which goes against the person's
own sexual inclinations.

But attractive as it may be for some, this view cannot
be supported by the text itself. The words for "natural"
and "against nature" do not describe our subjective experience of what feels natural to us, but instead refer to
the fixed way of things in creation. The nature that Paul
says homosexual behavior contradicts is God's purpose

for us, revealed in creation and reiterated throughout Scripture.

This shows us why it is not true for those with SSA to say: "But God made me this way!" Paul's point in Romans 1 is that our "nature" (as we experience it) is not natural (as God intended it). All of us have desires that are warped as a result of our fallen nature. Desires for things God has forbidden are a reflection of how sin has distorted me, not of how God has made me.

Paul's reference to lesbianism as well as male homosexual conduct also confirms the idea that he is condemning *all* homosexual activity, and not just the man-boy relationships that are known to have occurred in Roman culture.

The strength of Paul's language here should not make us think that homosexual conduct is the worst or only form of sinful behavior. Paul may be highlighting it because it is a particularly vivid example, and may have been especially pertinent for his readers in Rome, given their cultural context. Either way it illustrates something that is the case for all of us: as we reject God, we find ourselves craving what we are not naturally designed to do. This is as true of a heterosexual person as of a homosexual person.

b. Homosexuality is a sign of God's judgment

Paul writes that alongside the gospel: "The wrath of God is being revealed from heaven against all the godlessness and wickedness of people" (Romans 1 v 18). Though there will one day be a "day of God's wrath, when his righteous judgment will be revealed" (Romans

2 v 5), there is already a present-day expression of God's anger against sin.

When we try to visualize what God's wrath looks like, many of us imagine CGI from a disaster movie, or think of lightning bolts falling from the sky. But Paul gives us a very different picture. We see God's wrath in this: *he gives us what we want.*

In response to the exchanges Paul has described, we see three instances of God *giving us over* to live in the outcome of our sinful desires. This is his present-day judgment against sin. We ask for a reality without him and he gives us a taster of it.

In each case the "giving over" results in an intensification of the sin and the further breakdown of human behavior. God gives humanity over to impure lusts and dishonorable bodily conduct (v 24), and to "shameful lusts" (v 26). The exchanging of natural relations for unnatural ones leads to being given over to a "depraved mind" and the flourishing of "every kind of wickedness," which Paul unpacks in a long list of antisocial behaviors (v 28-31). Sin leads to judgment, but judgment also leads to further sin.

The presence of all these sinful acts is a reminder that we live in a world experiencing a foretaste of God's anger and provoking its final outpouring on the day of judgment. That homosexual activity is listed among these acts indicates that it is, in itself, testimony to the warped nature of sinful humanity.

It is important to recognize that Paul is talking in societal rather than individual terms. He is describing what happens to culture as a whole, rather than particular people. The presence of same-sex desire in some of us is not an indication that we have turned from God more than others, or have been given over by God to further sin more than others.

There is a parallel with suffering. The presence of particular suffering in someone's life does not mean they've sinned more than someone suffering less. Rather, the presence of suffering anywhere is an indication that as a race we are under God's judgment. Similarly, the presence of homosexual feelings in me reminds me that my desires are not right because the world is not right. Together we have turned from God and together we have been given over to sin.

4. 1 Corinthians 6 v 9-10

> Or do you not know that the unrighteous will not inherit the kingdom of God? Do not be deceived: neither the sexually immoral, nor idolaters, nor adulterers, nor men who practice homosexuality, nor thieves, nor the greedy, nor drunkards, nor revilers, nor swindlers will inherit the kingdom of God. *1 Corinthians 6 v 9-10, ESV*

In these verses Paul is describing different kinds of people who (unless they repent) will be excluded from the kingdom of God. Four kinds relate to sexual sin, and two of those specifically to homosexual behavior. The ESV takes the latter and puts them together as "men who practice homosexuality," while the NIV 1984 translates them as "male prostitutes and homosexual offenders."

The stakes are high: Paul is giving examples of people who will not be in heaven. We need to make sure we understand exactly what he is talking about.

The first of the two terms relating to homosexuality is *malakoi*, which literally means those who are "soft." In classical literature it could be used as a pejorative term for men who were effeminate; for the younger, passive partner in a pederastic (man-boy) relationship; or to refer to male prostitutes (hence the NIV 1984's translation). In 1 Corinthians 6 *malakoi* comes in a list describing general forms of sexual sin, and this context suggests Paul is most likely using it in a broad way to refer to the passive partners in homosexual intercourse.

This also fits Paul's pairing of *malakoi* with the second term he uses. *Arsenokoitai* is a compound of "male" (*arsen*) and "intercourse" (*koites*, literally "bed"). These are the two words used in the Greek translation of Leviticus 18 v 22 and 20 v 13, suggesting that Paul is referring back to those two passages.

Arsenokoitai, then, is a general term for same-sex sex, and its pairing with *malakoi* indicates that Paul is addressing both the active and passive partners in homosexual sex.

So what does all this mean for our understanding of homosexuality?

Homosexual sin is serious. Paul says that the active and unrepentant homosexual (as with all the unrighteous) will not enter God's kingdom. This is a very stark truth.

Paul also reminds his readers not to be deceived on this point. He assumes there will be those who deny this teaching, and argue that some forms of homosexual conduct are acceptable to God. But Paul is clear: homosexual conduct leads people to destruction. To teach otherwise (as a number of purportedly Christian leaders sadly do) is tantamount to sending people to hell. This is a gospel issue (see the box on page 73).

Homosexual sin is not unique. Paul's list includes other forms of sexual sin (sexual immorality and adultery), and it includes non-sexual forms of sin (drunkenness and theft, for example). Homosexual sin is incredibly serious, but it is not alone in being so. It is wicked, but so is greed. God will judge those who indulge in it. But he will also judge thieves.

So we must never imply that homosexuality is the sin of our age. If we are to be faithful to Scripture, we must also preach against theft, greed, drunkenness, reviling, and defrauding others, many of which are also trivialized in western society, and all of which also characterize the unrighteous. But there is a wonderful promise in this passage too:

Homosexual sin is not inescapable

Paul continues in verse 11:

> *And that is what some of you were.* But you were washed, you were sanctified, you were justified in the name of the Lord Jesus Christ and by the Spirit of our God.   *1 Corinthians 6 v 11*

These forms of behavior are not appropriate for the Corinthian Christians precisely because *it is not who they are anymore*. Some of them clearly had been active homosexuals. They did once live in these ways. *But no more*. They have been washed, sanctified and justified; forgiven, cleansed from their sins, and set apart for God. They have a new standing and identity before him.

However ingrained it may be in someone's behavior, homosexual conduct is not inescapable. It is possible for someone living a practicing gay lifestyle to be made new by God. Temptations and feelings may well linger. That Paul is warning his readers not to revert to their former way of life suggests there is still some desire to. But in Christ we are no longer who we were. Those who have come out of an active gay lifestyle need to understand how to see themselves. What defined us then no longer defines us now.

5. 1 Timothy 1 v 9-10

> We also know that the law is made not for the righteous but for lawbreakers and rebels, the ungodly and sinful, the unholy and irreligious, for those who kill their fathers or mothers, for murderers, for the sexually immoral, for those practicing homosexuality, for slave traders and liars and perjurers—and for whatever else is contrary to the sound doctrine.   *1 Timothy 1 v 9-10*

Paul again uses the term *arsenokoitai* (translated by the ESV as "men who practice homosexuality" and by the NIV 1984 as "perverts") as a catch-all term for all forms of homosexual conduct. Also, in common with 1 Corinthians, same-sex sex is mentioned among other wide-ranging sins, non-sexual as well as sexual.

These forms of behavior characterize those who are not "just," and for whom the law was given in order to bring conviction of sin and the need for mercy. All these practices contradict "sound doctrine" and the gospel. They do not conform to the life Christians are now to lead. They go against the grain of the new identity we have in Christ.

This will have been a hard chapter for many of us to read. It was not an easy chapter to write! In each instance where the Bible directly addresses homosexual behavior it is to condemn it. The consistent teaching of the Bible is clear: God forbids homosexual activity. Given what the Bible says about God's purpose of sex and marriage, this should not surprise us.

In fact, the situation is worse than many people might think. God is opposed to all sexual activity outside of heterosexual marriage. It's not that the Bible opposes all homosexual activity but approves of any and every sexual act between heterosexual people.

But for those who experience homosexual feelings themselves, or for those who are close to people who do, these teachings in the Bible can be very hard indeed. And it can feel particularly hard for those of us who are Christian and yet find ourselves experiencing SSA. What does that mean for us? Do these feelings write us off as Christians?

The answer, wonderfully, is "no!" *Let's find out why in the next chapter.*

Surely a same-sex partnership is OK if it's committed and faithful?

One of the arguments commonly made today in favor of same-sex partnerships is that what must surely count above all else is faithfulness and commitment. Shouldn't faithfulness within a relationship be what determines its moral goodness rather than the gender of those involved in it? A promiscuous gay lifestyle with multiple partners and one-night stands might be wrong, but two people who love each other and are faithful to whatever promises they have made—surely that's OK?

It can seem a compelling argument, and it is increasingly common to find Christians allowing for this kind of expression of homosexual practice. But a number of important things need to be said in response.

In 1 Corinthians 5 Paul rebukes the Corinthian church for its acceptance of an illicit relationship. A man is in a relationship with his father's wife, most likely his stepmother—an arrangement expressly forbidden in Leviticus 18. Paul is dismayed. Even the pagans in Corinthian society would not allow such a thing (1 Corinthians 5 v 1), and yet here it is going on in plain sight among God's people.

Paul's response to this situation is instructive, as much for what he doesn't say as for what he does say. There is no question about whether this particular couple love each other. Paul does not ask about their level of commitment or whether they are being faithful. That is not the issue. Whether or not they are in a long-term committed relationship is beside the point; the fact remains that it is wrong and should not be happening.

Paul does not distinguish between faithful illicit relationships and profligate illicit relationships, as if the latter are out of bounds but the former might just squeak in by virtue of their faithfulness. Consistency and faithfulness while sinning in no way diminish the sin. Paul calls for the church member in question to be expelled from the fellowship, and for the whole church to express remorse at what has happened (1 Corinthians 5 v 2). Faithfulness demonstrated in an otherwise prohibited relationship does not make it less sinful.

In many areas of life it is possible to demonstrate good qualities while doing something wrong. A thief in a gang may demonstrate impeccable loyalty to his fellow gang members during the act of stealing: looking out for them, protecting them from danger, being sure to give them a generous proportion of the takings. None of this in any way lessens the immorality of the act; it just means he is being a "good" thief rather than a "bad" thief. As we have seen, Scripture is clear in its prohibition of any homosexual activity. Activity that is faithful and commited is no more permissible than activity that's promiscuous and unfaithful.

But Jesus never mentions homosexuality, so how can it be wrong?

It is sometimes said that since Jesus never mentioned homosexuality directly, he can't have been against it. But although Jesus does not directly mention homosexuality, in his teaching on sexual sin he does address it. Consider the following:

What comes out of a person is what defiles them. For it is from within, out of a person's heart, that evil thoughts come—sexual immorality, theft, murder, adultery, greed, malice, deceit, lewdness, envy, slander, arrogance and folly. All these evils come from inside and defile a person.
Mark 7 v 20-23

Jesus says there are things that make someone spiritually unclean before God. In this list Jesus includes (among other things) examples of sexual sin: adultery, lewdness and sexual immorality. "Sexual immorality" translates a Greek word, *porneia* (from which we get the word "pornography"), something of a catch-all term for any sexual activity outside of marriage. This extends beyond intercourse to include any activity of a sexual nature. None of Jesus' hearers would have doubted that his reference to *porneia* included homosexual behavior.

Imagine that at my church this Sunday I decide, in a moment of impetuous and uncharacteristic generosity, to thank everyone attending by offering them a free gift of £1,000. Everyone in the building is eligible and just needs to come and see me at the door. Now, if you are there when I make that promise, you are included in it. I haven't mentioned your name; I haven't addressed you directly. But I have included you. In his prohibitions against sexual immorality Jesus doesn't name homosexuality, but he does include it.

One further point needs to be made. As well as condemning sexual sin outside marriage, Jesus indicated that the only godly alternative to marriage was celibacy. In Matthew 19, when Jesus had outlined God's purpose for human marriage, his disciples responded in exasperation: "If this is the situation between a husband and wife, it is better not to marry" (Matthew 19 v 10). They think that Jesus' teaching is a bitter pill to swallow. If marriage is that big a deal, they think, maybe it's better to steer clear of the whole thing.

Jesus' response to them is significant:

> Not everyone can accept this word, but only those to whom it has been given. For there are eunuchs who were born that way, and there are eunuchs who have been made eunuchs by others—and there are those who choose to live like eunuchs for the sake of the kingdom of heaven. The one who can accept this should accept it.
> **Matthew 19 v 11-12**

Eunuchs were the celibates of their day, and Jesus indicates that their celibacy might be the result of birth, or human intervention, or a voluntary decision to forego marriage. Whatever its cause, that Jesus goes there right after his disciples have baulked at the commitment and seriousness of marriage shows that Jesus regards it as the only alternative.

One marries, or remains single.

There is no third possibility, whether of a homosexual partnership or a heterosexual unmarried partnership. As far as Jesus is concerned, the godly alternatives before us are (heterosexual) marriage or celibacy.

Chapter 3

Homosexuality and the Christian

We should expect a number of Christians to experience forms of same-sex attraction. We live in a fallen world. Creation has been affected by our sin. It has been subjected to frustration (Romans 8 v 20). There is sickness. There is disorder. It affects our bodies, our hearts, and our minds as well. Christians succumb to the ravages of this fallen order as much as anyone. Being Christian makes us no less likely to fall ill, face tragedy, or experience insecurity. All of us experience fallen sexual desires, whether those desires are heterosexual or homosexual by nature. It is not un-Christian to experience same-sex attraction any more than it is un-Christian to get sick. What marks us out as Christian is not that we never experience such things, but how we respond to them when we do.

So what of a Christian who finds themselves experiencing same-sex attraction? How should they respond? A number of things need to be encouraged.

1. Pray

Christians experiencing same-sex attraction need to talk to the Lord about it. It is important to know that it is an issue we can talk to our heavenly Father about. Homosexual feelings do not exclude us from his presence. The subject is not off-limits. He is no less our Father, and we are no less his beloved children, because we might experience something like this.

a. We can talk to God about any confusion and distress we might be feeling

We may not know where such feelings have come from or what they might mean for the future. But God knows us fully. We can take great comfort in the fact that he is in complete control, and that *in all things* (including unwanted experiences like this) he is working for our good. He promises to give us wisdom when we lack it— "generously to all without finding fault" (James 1 v 5). He is the first and best person to go to in any confusion and distress.

b. We can talk to God about our temptations

Jesus taught us to pray to the Father for deliverance from temptation (Matthew 6 v 13). It can be a helpful thing to articulate and confess in prayer the specific nature of our temptations. God is the one who gives us the strength to stand under them. Moreover, Jesus himself is not "unable to empathize with our weaknesses" but "has been tempted in every way, just as we are—yet he did not sin" (Hebrews 4 v 15). He knows what it is to struggle with temptation, and can feel for us when we do. This makes him a great Savior to pray to. We can approach him with great confidence. He is not aloof or lacking in understanding.

c. We can also talk to God about our sins

There may be any number of ways in which we have succumbed to homosexual temptation in our thoughts or actions. It is right for such sins to weigh heavily on our hearts. *But we must rejoice that they are not unforgiveable.* Christ died no less for sins such as these. The apostle John reminds us that: "If we confess our sins, [God] is faithful and just and will forgive us our sins and purify us from all unrighteousness" (1 John 1 v 9). It is a wonderful blessing to know that we can talk to God about the very worst things we have done and thought.

2. Think about it in the right way

Christians need to think clearly about what these feelings do mean and don't mean.

a. They do not disqualify you

I have met many Christians who have said that their experiences of SSA have made them feel deeply and spiritually unclean. Some have spoken of feeling like "damaged goods," as though they were beyond repair and forever displeasing to God.

It is easy to make comparisons with those who experience heterosexual forms of temptation; at least they're being tempted by a form of sexual expression they were designed for. It can make those struggling with SSA feel doubly ashamed: not just tempted by a wrong thing, but a wrong kind of wrong thing.

There is a right recognition that this is not how we are meant to be. Such feelings provide a wonderful opportunity to be reminded of the gospel. We could never be acceptable to God on the basis of our own merits and actions. It has never been about us having intrinsic worth or natural spiritual cleanliness. Quite the opposite. It is only "in Christ" that anyone is righteous in God's sight (2 Corinthians 5 v 21). And, wonderfully, no experience of temptation, however unremitting it may seem, is ever a threat to that. In Christ we are presented holy and blameless in God's sight (Colossians 1 v 22).

b. They do not define you

It's easy to get these feelings out of proportion in another way: to think that they represent the sum total of our identity. We live in a culture where sexuality is virtually equated with identity: "You are your sexuality." We are encouraged to think that to experience homosexual feelings means that you are, at your most fundamental core, a homosexual.

It is very easy for Christians to lose a healthy perspective on this. We can think that SSA is *the* issue in our Christian life, as though no other sins or struggles warranted serious attention. My own perception is that I struggle with greed much more than I do with sexual temptation. But SSA can become the lens through which the whole of our Christian life is viewed. Yes, it has a significant effect on a number of defined areas of life, but it does not define your life.

As we have already seen, Paul can say of Christian men and women who were once practicing homosexuality: "That is what some of you were" (1 Corinthians 6 v 11). Some of the temptations may remain, but our identity has radically changed.

It is also important to understand that sexuality is not necessarily a static thing. Our desires at one stage of development may not be the same at another. This is perhaps especially true of puberty, when sexual attractions can change considerably. I have met many men and women who have been through periods of SSA in teenage years, only to discover that their desires eventually reverted to opposite-sex attraction. In the developmental course of events, once-SSA does not necessarily mean always-SSA; it is all the more important that someone experiencing SSA for the first time does not assume that this is now the "orientation" they are to live with for the rest of their life.

3. Seek the support of others

Talking with others can be very hard. If we have only ever heard homosexuality being spoken of in strongly negative terms in church, then we may feel uneasy about speaking to other believers about our own experiences of homosexual feelings.

Sometimes Christians experiencing SSA feel as if they are letting the side down by having these feelings, or that their Christian friends and even pastors will be disappointed in them. But we are never letting anyone down when we share a struggle. Actually, it is an enormous privilege to have another Christian share a personal struggle with us. All of us are weak! No Christian is designed to struggle alone. All Christians need the support of others. We are called to "carry each other's burdens," and so "fulfill the law of Christ" (Galatians 6 v 2).

Can God change our sexual desires?

In one sense the answer to this question is a very unambiguous "yes!" We know that in Christ we have the future hope of eternity in the new creation, where we will no longer experience the temptations and consequences of sin. We will have renewed bodies. There will be no more tears. All distress will have gone. There will be no more struggles with sexuality. In eternity, we will be changed forever to be like Christ. That is the Christian's sure hope.

But what of this life? Is it possible that God *might* change our sexual desires before we reach the new creation?

I believe that change is possible, but a complete change of sexual orientation is never promised in the Bible.

Christians believe that God is sovereign, and therefore that he is able to heal us by the work of his Holy Spirit, even in this life, from any brokenness we have experienced, and also deliver us from any negative patterns of behavior. There should be no doubt that God *can* change our sexual desires, and there are numerous accounts of when he has done just that.

I think of a good friend of mine who saw his sexual desires change quickly and dramatically. As a young

Christian man he experienced exclusively homosexual desires. It was as he was beginning to come to terms with this, and had started sharing this fact with family and friends, that he found himself changing very quickly. He fell in love with a woman he knew and has now been happily married to her for many years. He has experienced virtually no homosexual feelings since then. He hadn't been actively seeking change, but it came anyway. I have read and heard of other Christians who have experienced a similar level of change, though not necessarily as suddenly.

But this has not been a universal experience. There are Christians who have prayed fervently for change and experienced it; there are others who have prayed equally fervently but have not.

We need to remember that as Christians we live between two realities:

1. When we become Christians we are made new

If anyone is in Christ, he is a new creation.
2 Corinthians 5 v 17, ESV

We have been given a new self (Ephesians 4 v 24). The gospel has brought not just a change *in* us, but a change *of* us. We have been made new or, to use the language of Jesus, we have been born again (John 3 v 3).

2. But we have not yet received the fullness of our salvation as God's people

We still wait for our "adoption to sonship" and "the

redemption of our bodies" (Romans 8 v 23). We continue our struggle with sin. Temptation does not cease. The full healing and deliverance we long for are not promised this side of the new creation.

It is for this reason—being caught between these two realities—that Paul says we groan (Romans 8 v 23). We have tasted our sonship and therefore we long for it in all its fullness—like being given a spoonful of a delicious meal that is being prepared for you and realizing at once just how hungry you are and how wonderful it will be to sit down at the table and eat your fill.

There are times when God graciously pours part of our future reality back into our present-day experience and provides radical healing and deliverance. Such occasions dramatically demonstrate God's power over other forces in our lives. We give thanks to God when this happens. But God is *also* glorified as we learn to rejoice in him even when affliction remains and change seems to be very slow—or when it feels as if we are going backwards.

Change in this life is possible but not promised. So we should not presume that it could never happen, or that it must happen. We must learn to trust the God who knows the end from the beginning, and always does precisely what is right.

Can we really expect unmarried Christians with same-sex attraction to remain single?

We have already seen that the Bible prohibits any sexual activity outside of heterosexual marriage. It will be possible for some Christians with SSA to marry. This may be because they experience a measure of change in their sexual desires, or else because they find that, despite on-going homosexual temptation, they are able to enjoy a happy marriage to someone of the opposite sex.

I think of a number of women and men I know for whom this has been the case. Their desires remain pre-dominantly homosexual, but they have nevertheless found deep companionship and sufficient (if not exact-ly "off the charts") sexual chemistry in a heterosexual marriage.

But what about brothers and sisters for whom marriage will be unrealistic? Is singleness required? Is it realistic?

The Bible's answer to both these questions is *"yes."*

As already discussed, when Jesus talks about the al-ternative to marriage, he does not mention cohabita-tion, same-sex partnerships or any other kind of sexual relationship. He mentions the eunuchs—the celibate (Matthew 19 v 10-12). This is the only godly alternative to heterosexual marriage. For as long as someone is un-married, they must abstain from sexual activity. "Celi-bate" and "chaste" are somewhat old-fashioned words, but they capture the sort of thing being spoken about: single and sexually abstinent.

Healthy singleness

But is this healthy? In our day and age, where free sex-ual expression is encouraged, can we expect unmarried people to refrain from all sexual behavior?

In one sense the question is answered for us imme-diately if we are already commited to the authority of the Bible. God's word is clear. If we follow the Bible, we must adhere to it on this point. It will not do to claim to be Bible-believing (the position of mainline Christianity throughout church history), but then reject particular teachings at our own discretion. That would make us, and not God, decide what is truth.

The Bible tells us the positives of singleness. There may be different reasons why someone would be single long-term (as Jesus himself acknowledges with the eunuchs in Matthew 19), but in each case it can be a means of blessing, both to ourselves and others.

Paul speaks of being single as a "gift" from God (1 Corinthians 7 v 7), to be understood alongside the gift of being married. Singleness is not just the absence of marriage, but is a good and blessed thing in and of itself. Each state (married and single) has its own ups and downs, opportunities and challenges, griefs and joys.

The Bible is very positive about singleness. Jesus himself was single, and this is very significant. He was the most fully human and complete person who ever lived. His singleness in no way diminished his humanity. He was not less of a person for it. No one is. Marriage, for all its blessings, is not intrinsic to being whole and fully realized as a person.

Singleness has certain advantages. Paul says what is obvious: that the single person is spared certain "troubles in this life" (1 Corinthians 7 v 28). Marital and family life can be hard, at times incredibly so. There are many time- and energy-sapping responsibilities for a married Christian and parent.

As a pastor I get to spend a lot of time with a range of families, both inside and outside the church. At times it makes me broody—joining in with a family game, helping kids with homework, having the newborn baby fast asleep on my shoulder. I can find myself pining for a family of my own.

But at other times the exact opposite is true! I walk unsuspecting through the front door only to discover World War Three has broken out in the household. There's yelling, mess, and hot tears being shed. I feel tense and awkward just being there. I try to calculate how short a time I can stay before it looks rude to leave. (Twelve minutes is about right, especially if you are able to tell them you're off to make another pastoral visit.)

At such times I am quietly thankful for the gift of singleness!

Singleness also provides particular opportunities. The single person, Paul says, is less divided in their devotion to God (1 Corinthians 7 v 32-35). In all the complexity of family life, what devotion to the Lord looks like is not always straightforward—you are pulled in so many different directions at once. But for a single Christian it might be much clearer. Service and ministry can be approached whole-heartedly.

Single people often have a greater capacity for friendship, greater flexibility of lifestyle, and are free to serve in a greater range of ministries than might be the case with their married friends. As a single man, I am grateful that I have been able to drop everything to spend time with friends in great need. It has meant the world to me to be able to do that, and it would not have been so easy if I were married. I'm thankful, too, for the wide range of good friendships I have been able to cultivate.

It is a privilege to be involved in the lives of many other people in this way.

The blessing of singleness

Those of us who are single must make the most of the opportunities singleness provides for deepening and expressing our devotion to God. Far from being a shackle, singleness can be a wonderful blessing, both to us and to others. For those who are single long-term, the challenges and opportunities will change over time. Singleness in your 20s is a very different experience to singleness in your 50s. Some things will get more difficult; others will get easier. The kind of support we will need from others, and the kind of support we can be to others, might change considerably over the years.

The history of the church is filled with lifelong singles who have been an enormous blessing to God's people and the wider world. Some through missionary activity, others through church ministry, and others through faithful friendship and support to others. What an honor to be used in such a way.

What are the main struggles for a homosexual Christian?

Different people struggle in different ways. Not all the struggles of a Christian with SSA are unique to those wrestling with this issue. But the following are often mentioned as particular difficulties for those battling with homosexual feelings.

Loneliness: While there are often church events and groups that single people can enjoy, the social life of a church can often feel as though it is structured around couples and families. Single people can feel a little like spare parts, particularly if they are at a stage in life when most of their peers have married.

Some find it hard to know what to do with holidays; people tend to go away with their families or with other couples and families. I think of one Christian brother who often finds himself run down due to overwork, but says he overworks because it is just too painful to think about having to spend time off by himself.

It's easier to fill the day with work and ministry. He says he dreads others asking him what his plans are for the holidays. For others the difficulty is the experience of coming back home each day to an empty house. Not being the main person in someone else's life or having someone who will be thinking of you in a special way. As I heard one Christian sister say: "I just want to be first for someone!" Others have said they dread their birthdays, because of the absence of someone who will make them feel special.

This is often related to **isolation**. Single Christians often miss companionship: having people to "do nothing" with. One of the kindest gifts I received was from a family I popped round to visit quite often. I was about to move away and as a leaving present they gave me a small, wrapped box. What was inside was neither big nor expensive, and yet meant the world to me: a spare key to their house. It was a wonderful affirmation.

Sexual temptation: Sexual temptation of one kind or another is a struggle for most Christians, and a particular struggle for many. Experiencing SSA does not make sexual temptation either more or less pronounced than for anyone else. But it can be a difficult matter, especially if there's no one to talk it through with. Any battle faced in isolation is harder.

Experiencing SSA does not necessarily mean you will find yourself attracted to every person of the same gender that you come across, any more than heterosexual people are attracted to everyone they meet. But there can be times of deep attraction with particular friends.

For some, the attraction is more emotional than physical. I know a number of individuals with SSA who struggle with unhealthy emotional dependency on others. It can be agonizing when an otherwise great friendship starts to become the object of intense and unwanted longing. One friend described the experience as like taking "friendship heroin": finding yourself suddenly "high" when being affirmed by a particular friend, and then feeling a crushing sense of absence when apart from them. Needless to say, at such times it is vital to have others who will help, support and talk it through.

How can this be part of God's purposes?

The Bible assures us that: "In all things God works for the good of those who love him" (Romans 8 v 28). Those "all things" include the sinful tendencies we find ourselves struggling with, and even the mistakes we make in relation to them. "All things" includes things that would not be here if it were not for the fall, and which will not be present in the new creation, and yet which in the here and now God is able to use to bring good. Paul is not vague about what this goodness looks like. Our good is our becoming like Jesus:

> And we know that in all things God works for the good of those who love him, who have been called according to his purpose. For those God foreknew he also predestined to be conformed to the image of his Son, that he might be the firstborn among many brothers and sisters.   *Romans 8 v 28-29*

God's good plan is for there to be a vast crowd of people like Christ. This is the good into which he is pressing all things. It is a great comfort for a Christian struggling with unwanted SSA to know that in God's hands, such struggles can become a means of God's grace.

Paul knew something of this from his own experience. In 2 Corinthians 12 he speaks of bearing a "thorn in the flesh":

> Therefore, in order to keep me from becoming conceited, I was given a thorn in my flesh, a messenger of Satan, to torment me. Three times I pleaded with the Lord to take it away from me. But he said to me, "My grace is sufficient for you, for my power is made perfect in weakness."
> *2 Corinthians 12 v 7-9*

Paul does not tell us exactly what this "thorn" was. It may have been a chronic ailment, a recurring form of temptation, or perhaps a difficult individual. We don't know. But he does tell us it was unbearable. He "plead-ed" for it to be removed.

He also speaks of where it came from. It was from God—it was "given" to stop Paul from becoming conceited. And it was to God that Paul turned in pleading for it to be removed. Yet Paul also describes it as "a messenger of Satan," whose purpose was "to torment." It was clearly in and of itself not a good thing. And yet God's purpose was for it to remain in Paul's life and for goodness to come from it. God's will for him was for something greater even than relief from this torment: an appreciation of the all-sufficiency of God's grace.

Such passages provide great encouragement to those wrestling with SSA. For some the battle may be acutely painful. For some it may last for many long years. But in God's purposes it is not a wasted experience. Through it we can be made more like Christ, and better able to grasp the vast dimensions of his grace. There is nothing better for us than that. And so a "win" for Christians struggling with SSA is not that the temptations would go away, but that in the heat of them Jesus would be prized more and more.

Struggling with homosexual feelings is just that—a struggle. But many Christians I know can testify to how God has brought good things out of their experiences. Some have said that the Lord has made them more compassionate and sensitive than they might otherwise have been. Others speak of ministry opportunities it has given them, and of how they have been able to support and encourage others they know who are trying to deal with SSA. Some have had opportunities to share their faith with parts of the gay community that would be unreachable by conventional church witness. But perhaps above all they can say how these struggles, with all the disorder and insecurity that can come with them, have led to a deeper appreciation of how unfathomably good God is.

Aren't we just picking and choosing which Old Testament laws apply?

And the pig, though it has a divided hoof, does not chew the cud; it is unclean for you.
Leviticus 11 v 7

Do not wear clothes of wool and linen woven together. **Deuteronomy 22 v 11**

Do not have sexual relations with a man as one does with a woman; that is detestable.
Leviticus 18 v 22

It seems inconsistent of Christians to oppose homosexuality while ignoring many other rules in the Bible concerning matters like diet and what we wear. On the surface, it looks like a very strong argument. I just had pork for lunch and am writing this while wearing a shirt made from mixed fibers; both of these things were forbidden to God's people in the Old Testament.

The problem with this objection is that it assumes Christians have exactly the same approach to every part of the Old Testament law. In fact, the proper

Christian view of the Old Testament is a little more nuanced than that.

The Old Testament is not a flat landscape. It is not just a line-up of instructions and regulations, each of which is equally binding. It has a particular shape to it, a shape whose contours, emphases and priorities are outlined and filled in by Jesus himself, who said:

> Do not think that I have come to abolish the Law or the Prophets; I have not come to abolish them but to **fulfill** them.   **Matthew 5 v 17**

Jesus has not come to discard the law as nonsense from a bygone age, or to enforce it and police it. Nor has he come to fulfill just *bits* of it, sifting through the pile with a pair of tweezers and picking out the occasional commandment that might still work for us. What Jesus came to do with the law he came to do with *all of it.* But as we follow Jesus' life and ministry, it becomes apparent that he fulfills the various elements to the law in a variety of ways.

Jesus ended the cleanliness and food laws. He declared all foods clean (Mark 7 v 19, reiterated in Acts 10 v 9-16). He touched lepers and dead bodies, and was not made unclean by doing so.

He spoke of his body as the true temple and his death as the ultimate sacrifice for sin (John 2 v 21; Luke 22 v 19-20). His death opened the way for us to approach God, making Old Testament regulations concerning the temple and its sacrificial system obsolete.

Jesus re-made the people of God. In the Old Testament they were a nation-state. In the New they are a universal church embodied in numerous local gatherings around the world and subject to the laws of secular governments. The OT laws relating to the civic life of God's people (such as requiring the death penalty for grave sins) therefore no longer apply to believers today in the same way.

Through his sinless life Jesus fully embodied all the moral requirements of the law. Through union with him, the "righteous requirement of the law [is] fully met in us" as we live by the power of his Spirit (Romans 8 v 4). It is in this way that we're able to live lives of love, which is precisely what the moral laws of the OT were pointing to (Romans 13 v 8). In order to unpack what it means for us to live in love, many of the moral commandments of the OT are re-stated in the New, including those relating to sexual ethics.

Timothy Keller sums it up neatly: *In short, the coming of Christ changed how we worship, but not how we live. The moral law outlines God's own character—his integrity, love, and faithfulness. And so all the Old Testament says about loving our neighbor, caring for the poor, generosity with our possessions, social relationships, and commitment to our family is still in force. The New Testament continues to forbid killing or committing adultery, and all the sex ethic of the Old Testament is re-stated throughout the New Testament (Matthew 5 v 27-30; 1 Corinthians 6 v 9-20; 1 Timothy 1 v 8-11). If the New Testament has reaffirmed a commandment, then it is still in force for us today.*[1]

---

1   Timothy Keller, "Old Testament Law and The Charge of Inconsistency," Redeemer Report, June 2012, http://www.redeemer.com/news_and_events/newsletter/?aid=363. Accessed 12/11/12.

We do not honor all the Old Testament texts in the same way. We take our cue from Jesus. It is because of what he claimed his death would achieve that we do not follow all Old Testament laws. To do so would be to undermine his work on the cross. So the Old Testament's teaching on sexual ethics, through it's restatement in the New Testament, is still binding on Christians today.

Is it sinful to experience same-sex attraction?

Same-sex attraction is not a good thing. It is (along with many other things) a consequence of the fall. It did not exist before the fall in Genesis 3 and it will not exist in the new creation. This kind of attraction is not something God designed for us, and it contradicts his design.

We know from the Scriptures that temptation comes from our own fallen hearts. James is very clear on this:

> When tempted, no one should say, "God is tempting me." For God cannot be tempted by evil, nor does he tempt anyone; but each person is tempted when they are dragged away by their own evil desire and enticed.   *James 1 v 13-14*

We cannot blame temptation on anyone else, certainly not God. Homosexual temptations reflect our own fallenness.

But this is not the same as saying *the presence of temptation itself* is a sin to be repented of. Christians have always made a distinction between temptation and sin. After all, Jesus himself taught his followers to pray:

> Forgive us our debts, as we also have forgiven our debtors. And lead us not into temptation, but deliver us from the evil one.
> *Matthew 6 v 12-13*

In other words, we seek forgiveness for sin and deliverance from temptation. We are not asked to seek forgiveness for being tempted, but only for any sin committed when we succumb to it. Instead, we are called to stand up under temptation, to endure it faithfully (1 Corinthians 10 v 13).

At the very moment we experience inappropriate attraction toward someone of the same sex, then we are to resist impure thoughts and emotions that we may be encountering, acknowledge that we want to flee from such things and not embrace them, and seek his help and strength to do so. We remember that such experiences are not God's design for us and therefore not good for us. We fight to honor God, trusting that he is faithful and will not allow us to be tempted beyond what we can bear.

To say that the very experience of SSA is a sin seems to suggest that even having the capacity to be tempted is itself a sin, something that I do not believe Scripture says.

And as we would expect, saying something that is unscriptural can cause significant pastoral damage. Many Christians experiencing SSA feel intense shame as a result. They know these feelings are not part of God's design, they long not to have them, and they strive to be obedient to Christ. In my experience, Christians with SSA typically feel deeper shame over their sexual temptations than their opposite-sex-attracted counterparts. To hear that the very presence of this temptation (irrespective of the extent to which they have endured faithfully under it) is *itself* a sin to be repented of might easily crush an already very tender believer.

Chapter 4

Homosexuality and the church

hen you think about it, church is an incredible thing. Sure, there are plenty of imperfections and limitations that we could focus on. And these might be particularly apparent for some of us thinking through the issue of homosexuality. The church has not always been a voice or place of love and grace.

It has been sad to hear from some friends struggling with SSA of instances where they have felt deep rejection from other Christians. For many churches there are no doubt lessons to learn and things to be repented of.

But for all its flaws, the church is remarkable. Listen to what Paul says:

> [God's] intent was that now, *through the church,*
> the manifold wisdom of God should be made
> known to the rulers and authorities in the heav-
> enly realms.   *Ephesians 3 v 10 [my emphasis]*

The church on earth is God's visual aid to the spiritual world of what he is like. It is by pointing to his people that God intends to show every spiritual power that he is wiser than any of them. But it is also a great encouragement to us. We must never underestimate the impact our Christian communities can have on others around us. Each church has a wonderful opportunity to point the world around it to the character and supreme wisdom of God. This is no less true when it comes to the area of homosexuality.

What should we do if a gay couple start coming to our church?

It's a great blessing and opportunity when any people start coming to church for the first time. Unless they are already Christians who have moved from another area or a different church, there is a wonderful opportunity for the church to introduce these newcomers to the gospel of Jesus. It makes no difference if they are a gay couple, a straight couple, or anybody else. All are sinners, and all need God's grace.

Sometimes there is the danger of Christians thinking that a gay couple need to be confronted with their sexuality almost the moment they walk through the door; that this needs to be talked about immediately and the couple told what the Bible's teaching is on the whole issue. This is simply not the case.

A comparison may help. If a heterosexual couple arrive at church and, upon welcoming them and chatting to them, it becomes apparent that they are living together but are unmarried, I wouldn't feel it necessary to immediately launch into a discussion about what the Bible says concerning the shortcomings of co-habitation. I would make a mental note that this will be an issue to think through with them in due course, but it doesn't need to be thrashed out for them to start participating regularly in the life of the church. If they bring it up, then of course I will respond. But my initial concern is for them to know they are welcome and that we are glad to have them with us, and for them to come under the sound of the gospel through the church's regular ministry.

Another way to put this is to say that I would rather start at the center and work outwards, than start at the edge and work in.

The center is the death and resurrection of Christ. That is where God reveals himself most fully. That is where we see his glory most clearly (John 17 v 1). It is also where God most clearly shows his love, righteousness, power, and wisdom (Romans 5 v 8; 3 v 25-26; 1 Corinthians 1 v 18, 24). This is what I most want people to know—for them to be bowled over by the God of the cross and resurrection. And, once they are gripped by this, to help them think through what trusting in this God will involve—what will need to be given over to him, including our messed-up sexuality.

But I want that conversation to take place in the context of the gospel, rather than start with their sexuality and try to get from there to the gospel. They need to know who Jesus is before being landed with what he requires. There is little point in describing how to live in the light of God's grace if someone doesn't yet know God's grace. So when a gay couple start coming to church, my priority for them is the same as for anyone else: to hear the gospel and experience the welcome of a Christian community.

What can the church do to support Christians facing this issue?

There are a number of things churches can do to help Christians with SSA:

1. Make it easy to talk about

Pastors as well as church members need to know that homosexuality is not just a political issue but a personal one, and that there will likely be some within their own church family for whom it is a painful struggle. When the issue comes up in the life of the church, it needs to be recognized that this is an issue Christians wrestle with too, and the church needs to be ready and equipped to walk alongside such brothers and sisters.

Many Christians still speak about homosexuality in hurtful and pejorative ways. I've lost count of the times I've heard Christians (even some in positions of church leadership) use phrases like: "That's so gay" to describe something they don't like. Such comments are only going to make their Christian brothers and sisters struggling with SSA feel completely unable to open up. When I first began to share my own experiences with friends at church, I was struck by how many mature Christians felt they needed to apologize for comments they'd made in the past about homosexuality, which they now realized may have been hurtful.

Key to helping people feel safe about sharing issues of SSA is having a culture of openness about the struggles and weaknesses we experience in general in the Christian life. Christian pastor and writer Timothy Keller has said that churches should feel more like the waiting room for a doctor and less like a waiting room for a job interview. In the latter we all try to look as competent and impressive as we can. Weaknesses are buried and hidden. But in a doctor's waiting room we assume that everyone there is sick and needs help. And this is much closer to the reality of what is going on in church.

By definition, Christians are weak. We depend on the grace and generosity of God. We are the "poor in spirit" (Matthew 5 v 3). It is a mark of a healthy church that we can talk about these things, and so we need to do all we can to encourage a culture of being real about the hard things of the Christian life.

But there is a caution: having made it easy for someone to talk about their sexual struggles, we must not then make the mistake of *always* talking to them about it. They may need to be asked about how things are going from time to time, but to make this the main or only thing you talk about with them can be problematic. It may reinforce the false idea that this is who they really are, and it may actually overlook other issues that they may need to talk about more. Sexuality may not be their greatest battle.

2. Honor singleness

Those for whom marriage is not a realistic prospect need to be affirmed in their calling to singleness. Our fellowships need to uphold and honor singleness as a gift and take care not unwittingly to denigrate it. Singles should not be thought or spoken of as loose ends that need tying up. Nor should we think that every single person is single because they've been too lazy to look for a marriage partner.

I remember meeting another pastor who, on finding out I was single, was insistent that I should be married by now and proceeded to outline immediate steps I needed to take to rectify this. He was very forthright and only backed down when I burst into tears and told him I was struggling with homosexuality. It is not an admission I should have needed to make. We need to respect that singleness is not necessarily a sign that someone is postponing growing up.

3. Remember that church is family

Paul repeatedly refers to the local church as "God's household" (for example, 1 Timothy 3 v 15). It is the family of God, and Christians are to be family to one another.

So Paul encourages Timothy to treat older men as fathers, "younger men as brothers, older women as mothers, and younger women as sisters" (1 Timothy 5 v 1-2). The church is to think of itself as immediate family. Nuclear families within the church need the input and involvement of the wider church family; they are not designed to be self-contained. Those that open up their family life to others find that it is a great two-way blessing.

Singles get to experience some of the joys of family life; children get to benefit from the influence of other older Christians; parents get to have the encouragement of others supporting them; and families as a whole get to learn something of what it means to serve Christ by being outward-looking as a family.

4. Deal with biblical models of masculinity and femininity, rather than cultural stereotypes

Battles with SSA can sometimes be related to a sense of not quite measuring up to expected norms of what a man or woman is meant to be like. So when the church reinforces superficial cultural stereotypes, the effect can be to worsen this sense of isolation and of not quite measuring up.

For example, to imply that men are supposed to be into sports or fixing their own car, or that women are supposed to enjoy craft or to suggest that they will want to "talk about everything," is to deal in cultural rather than biblical ideas of how God has made us. It can actually end up overlooking many ways in which people are reflecting some of the biblical aspects of manhood and womanhood that culture overlooks.

5. Provide good pastoral support

Pastoral care for those with SSA does not need to be structured, but *it does need to be visible.* Many churches now run support groups for members battling with SSA; others provide mentoring or prayer-partner schemes.

Those with SSA need to know that the church is ready to support and help them, and that it has people with a particular heart and insight to be involved in this ministry. There may be issues that need to be worked through, and passages from the Bible that need to be studied and applied with care and gentle determination. There may be good friendships that need to be cultivated and accountability put in place, and there will be the need for long-term community. These are all things the local church is best placed to provide.

It has been a few years now since I first started telling close Christian friends that I battle with homosexual feelings. It was a lengthy process and in some ways quite emotionally exhausting. But it was one of the best things I have ever done. The very act of sharing something so personal with someone else is a great trust, and in virtually every case it strengthened and deepened the friendship. Close friends have became even closer. I also found that people felt more able to open up to me about personal things in their own lives, on the basis that I had been so open with them. There have been some wonderful times of fellowship as a result.

It has also now been a few years since I shared about the issue of sexuality publicly with my church family. Again, it has been a great blessing to have done so. There has been a huge amount of support—people asking how they can help and encourage me in this issue, and many saying that they are praying for me daily. Others have said how much it means to them that I would share something like this. It has also been a great encouragement to me that it does not seem to have defined how others see me. Aside from the expressions of love and support, business was back to normal very quickly.

Some Christians (like many in my own church) seem

to know instinctively how to respond to fellow Christians battling with SSA. But the same is not necessarily true when it comes to responding to those outside the church who come out to us as being gay.

What is the right response then? How can Christians be salt and light to wider society on this kind of issue? This is the theme of the final chapter.

Can't Christians just agree to differ on this?

There are Christians and even leaders in churches today who argue that some forms of homosexual activity are acceptable to God, and many more who argue alongside me that any such activity is forbidden by God. In our churches and wider Christian communities we can differ on certain issues while keeping fellowship in the gospel. *So isn't homosexuality an issue over which Christians may legitimately disagree?*

The Bible allows for disagreements on certain issues. In Romans 14 Paul speaks about "disputable matters" and calls on his readers to be convinced in their own mind of what they think (Romans 14 v 5). But Paul also argues that there are other issues that are non-negotiable: issues where the gospel itself is at stake. In 1 Corinthians 15, he reminds his readers of the matters of "first importance" that he had earlier taught them and which stood at the heart of their gospel faith (1 Corinthians 15 v 1-11). Into which category does homosexuality fit? Does it affect the gospel? Two passages indicate that homosexuality is a gospel issue.

As we saw earlier, Paul talks about homosexual practice in the context of warning his readers that the un-righteous will not enter the kingdom of God (1 Corin-thians 6 v 9). In this category he includes those who practise homosexuality. Along with all who are unright-eous, such people are heading for destruction. Their only hope is the gospel, the outworking of which will include a new identity and repenting of their former lifestyle. To deny this truth has huge consequences. A church leader who teaches that even certain kinds of homosexual activity are OK is actually sending people to destruction. It is not the same order of disagreement as Christians have over, say, baptism, or the practice of certain spiritual gifts. In the case of homosexual prac-tice, the gospel is very much at stake.

In Revelation 2 v 20-21 Jesus rebukes the church in Thy-atira for their tolerance of a false teacher: *"I have this against you: You tolerate that woman Jezebel, who calls herself a prophet. By her teaching she misleads my servants into sexual immorality and the eating of food sacrificed to idols. I have given her time to repent of her immorality, but she is unwilling."*

This is someone whose teaching leads others in the church into sexual sin. Jesus promises judgment on her and any of her followers who do not repent (see v 22). But the responsibility lies not just with them. The church—including the many who do not follow her—are rebuked for tolerating her. So we are not to toler-ate in our churches those whose teaching leads people into sexual sin. They must be confronted, their ministry forbidden, and their teaching refuted. This is a gospel matter. If we allow this to be a matter of acceptable disagreement within our fellowships, Jesus will hold it against us. Some forms of tolerance are sinful.

Isn't the Christian view of sexuality dangerous and harmful?

One of the most common and significant charges leveled against the traditional Christian understanding of sexuality and marriage is that it is deeply damaging to individuals.

Denying someone's sexuality is seen as denying who that person really is. It is telling them to repress something central to their identity, and consequently, to their ability to flourish. This is harmful to anyone, but especially to teenagers who are coming to terms with their sexuality while still at a formative stage of their lives. Christians, it is claimed, are to blame for gay teenagers growing up stunted and guilt-ridden, or killing themselves.

This charge has perhaps been made most forcefully by Dan Savage:

> "The dehumanizing bigotry set forth from the lips of faithful Christians give your straight children a license to verbally abuse, humiliate, and condemn the gay children they encounter at school. They fill your gay children with suicidal despair. And you have the nerve to ask me to be more careful with my words." [1]

It goes without saying that this is an incredibly serious charge. It is troubling enough that many Christians are beginning to think the traditional understanding

---

1   Quoted in Justin Lee, *Torn: Rescuing The Gospel From The Gays-vs.-Christians Debate* Jericho Books, 2013, p.5

must be wrong if it is having this sort of effect on people. Surely anything that results in this kind of self-loathing and despair cannot be the fruit of God's truth.

The first thing to say in response to this is that there have certainly been instances of young people feeling driven to despair and even suicide in recent years, and attributing their distress to real or perceived pressure from Christian disapproval of homosexuality. This is a real situation. Young people both inside and outside the church are hurting profoundly on this issue.

And who can deny how unspeakably tragic it is that anyone should feel such despair over their own sexuality? Of all people, we Christians should feel most grief at this, knowing as we do the supreme value that God places on *all* human life. We should care more than anyone when we hear of young people in such torment—especially those growing up in Christian households and part of a local church.

And we must also recognize that some believers have undoubtedly been abusive in their behavior and language toward gay people, and thought that by being like this they were somehow advancing the cause of Christ. But we must also recognize that such behavior **is not itself Christian in any way**. It comes not by adhering to the message and example of Jesus, but by contradicting it.

But it is *not* true to say that such personal torment is the *inevitable* result of traditional biblical teaching on this issue. It is true that the convicting work of the Spirit can be very painful indeed. There is even a kind of self-loathing that can result when God makes us aware of the extent of our own sin (see Ezekiel 36 v 31). But though the genuine work of God might take us to such a place, it never leaves us there. If we are convicted, it is so that we can be restored. The Spirit breaks us only to put us back together as God intended. Jesus promises that we will find rest and comfort in him and that "a bruised reed he will not break" (Matthew 11 v 28-29; 12 v 20).

It is not the teaching of Jesus that tells you that life is not worth living if you can't be fulfilled sexually—that a life without sex is no life at all. It is not biblical Christianity that insists someone's sexual disposition is so foundational to who they are, and that to fail to affirm their particular leaning is to attack who that person is at their core. All this comes not from biblical Christianity but from western culture's highly distorted view of what it means to be a human. When an idol fails you, the real culprit turns out to be the person who has urged you worship it—not the person who has tried to take it away.

The teaching of Jesus does two things: it restricts sex and it relativizes its importance. Jesus shows us that in its God-given context the value of sex is far greater than we might have realized—and yet even there it is not ultimate. Sex is a powerful urge, but it is *not* fundamental to wholeness and human flourishing. Jesus showed that both in his teaching and in his lifestyle. After all, Jesus—the most fully human of all people—remained celibate himself.

The gospel shows us that there is forgiveness for all who have sinned sexually. And the gospel also liberates us from the mindset that sex is intrinsic to human fulfillment. The gospel call that no one need cast all their happiness on their sexual fortunes is not bad news but good news. *It is not the path to harm but to wholeness.*

Chapter 5

Homosexuality and the world

The Christian message is the best news that anyone can ever hope to hear. It's all about a God who is more forgiving and loving than we could possibly imagine. It's news we Christians want others to hear. But it is not always easy to share.

The gospel message has a number of sharp edges to it that many find difficult to hear. And these days one of the sharpest of those sharp edges seems to be what the Bible teaches about sexuality. It has led some Christians to change their mind about what the Bible says, in order to seem more accommodating and "relevant" to the outside world.

And while we might recognize that this is not a godly response to the issue, many Christians nevertheless still feel unsure about what we *should* do and say on this matter. We still sense that the gospel is for everyone, and that God's ways are the best ways. But how can we commend Christian thinking on this issue to the world around us?

My non-Christian friend has just told me they're gay. How should I respond?

Telling another person you're gay is normally a big deal for someone. If the person they're telling is a Christian, it is likely to be an even bigger deal. Many people assume Christians are anti-gay, and it is not a huge leap from that to think Christians must be against gay people themselves.

So the first thing you should do is **thank them** for being so open, and entrusting something so personal to you. It is a privilege to be told such things.

It is also important to **assure them that their fears of being rejected by you are unfounded**. Knowing they are gay should not mean you stop liking them or being their friend. In the interests of full disclosure—and especially if they ask you what you think about it—you might flag up that Christians have a different take on matters of sexuality than the culture does as a whole, and that you'd be happy to chat about that some time. But this may not be the moment.

Listen to them. It is good to ask people a bit about their experiences of homosexuality. How did they come to this realization about themselves? What kind of reactions have they had from other people—their friends and family? Has it been a hard time for them? Are they doing OK? We need to find out about their story and its ups and downs.

Understanding more of their background and experience will help us know how to be a good friend to them. They may need someone to listen to them from time to time, or be a shoulder to cry on, or be a friend they can speak to in confidence. Wouldn't it be great if, of all people, it was their Christian friend they felt most able to approach? Telling us about their sexuality could be an opportunity for the friendship to deepen rather than drift apart. And taking a genuine interest is more likely than anything else to prompt their questions about how we think about these matters as a believer.

Listening to them will help us know how to **pray for them**. Whatever their ups and downs, above all else—like any of us—they most need Christ. And as we pray for him to reveal his goodness to them, we can pray for ourselves, that our friendship would be a faithful expression of that goodness.

What's the best way to share Christ with a gay friend?

Because of the expectation gay friends will have about how Christians will respond to them, we need to make every effort to let them know that we are *for them* and not *against them*. This will at least involve taking time to get to know them well and listening carefully to their story. We need to love them more than their gay friends do, and we need to love *them* more than they love their homosexuality (as the Christian leader Al Mohler has put it). Only then can we begin to point to the greater love that God has for them.

At some point they will want to know what, as Christians, we make of homosexuality. We need to think carefully about how to explain this in a way that will be understood and appreciated, and not just met with defensiveness.

As important as explaining the particular truths of the Bible is explaining the reasons behind why it says them. So we will need to talk about how God cannot bless—and indeed forbids—homosexual activity, but we'll also want to show why God has a right to say what we should and shouldn't do with our bodies, and how it is we've come to see the goodness of what he says.

We will need to explain how repentance for the practicing homosexual will involve turning away from a gay lifestyle, but we'll also want to show how all of us, when we come to Christ, die to ourselves so that we can live a new life in him.

We will want to explain how the only appropriate lifestyle for those for whom marriage will not be realistic is chaste singleness, but we will also need to hold up a vision of how all of God's people—married and single alike—are pledged to one Husband, Christ (2 Corinthians 11 v 2); that any who unite themselves with Christ are one with him in spirit (1 Corinthians 6 v 17), and that this is the fundamental reality for all believers. Union with Christ forever is what the earthly states of both marriage and singleness actually point to. The purpose of earthly marriage is not to fulfill us, but to point us to the relationship that does. The purpose of singleness is not to show that we are sufficient, but to point us to the one who is. We will want gay friends to know that allegiance to Christ for a gay person is as costly and glorious as is it is for anyone else.

How can we be an effective witness to the world on this issue?

As western culture becomes ever more approving of homosexuality, it is going to feel more and more as though we Christians are failing in our attempts to commend a Christian view of sexuality. But we must not be disheartened.

The Bible assures us that Christ will build his church, and that his reign will forever increase (Matthew 16 v 18; Isaiah 9 v 7). This is no time for pessimism, and as society moves further and further away from its Christian moorings, the church is given more and more of an opportunity to model a counter-cultural alternative.

Key to our witness and credibility on this (or any) issue is the **quality of our life together**, and the **clarity of our message**. We need to be clear on the gospel. Clear that it is good news for everyone. That no one is too far gone to enjoy it, or too complete to need it. We need to be clear not just that we are all sinners, but that we are all sexual sinners. None of us are coming at this from any position of superiority.

With that gospel clarity needs to come **relational credibility**. The New Testament often connects the effectiveness of our witness with the genuineness of our love for one another. Jesus once said:

> By this everyone will know that you are my disciples, if you love one another.   *John 13 v 35*

Paul describes the church in the following way:

> God's household, which is the church of the living
> God, the pillar and foundation of the truth.
> *1 Timothy 3 v 15*

The church is the "pillar ... of the truth" because it is the outlet of God's truth into the world. It is God's means of bringing his truth to all people. But it is also God's family—his "household." And for the church to be an effective pillar, it needs to be an effective family. The local gathering of God's people is to embody the gospel in its own life. It is the church being church in all its biblical fullness that will most commend God's ways to wider society. Jesus' command that his followers "love one another" was not just an afterthought. It is a key part of his strategy to win a watching world.

Jesus promised that those with things to leave behind and give up for him will receive a hundredfold in return:

> "Truly I tell you," Jesus replied, "no one who has
> left home or brothers or sisters or mother or
> father or children or fields for me and the gospel
> will fail to receive a hundred times as much in this
> present age: homes, brothers, sisters, mothers,
> children and fields—along with persecutions—
> and in the age to come eternal life."
> *Mark 10 v 29-30*

The gospel can be relationally costly. But it is also relationally generous. What we leave behind does not compare with what we receive back from Jesus. It is hard to miss the fact that Jesus is talking about family. Close family. He doesn't promise distant cousins and great-uncles, but brothers and mothers. All that we have we are to share with one another: time, resources, affection. Ourselves. This, it turns out, is going to be the demonstration, in this life, that Jesus is always worth it. It will be the quality of our community life as church, as much as our ability to speak clearly into the public square, that will most visibly show a watching world that the Christian stance on sexuality is the most compelling.

Jesus's words give us all something to do. We might not have the best celebrities, the most attractive spokespeople, the most impressive resources or the most acclaimed thinkers, but we should have the most wonderful and attractive relationships.

Should Christians attend gay weddings?

As more and more parts of the western world legalize and promote same-sex marriage, Christians will increasingly find themselves in the position of being invited to gay weddings. *Should we go or not?*

We are meant, like Christ, to be a "friend of sinners," and should therefore strive to be the sort of friend someone would want to invite to their wedding. Figuring out what to do with such an invitation is therefore a good problem to have!

There are two very important aspects of our relationship with such friends that we must do all we can to preserve: our *witness* and our *friendship*.

First, we want to be careful as Christians not to appear to endorse something we understand to be a sin in God's eyes. Attending a gay wedding could easily look as if we are commending and celebrating gay marriage. It would be difficult to see how believers could attend without sending that kind of message. I know of some Christians who have attended simply to be a godly presence in an otherwise non-Christian environment, and who felt that their position on gay marriage had already been made sufficiently clear so as to avoid the risk of their attendance being misunderstood. But for many other Christians, it will not be possible to attend in good conscience.

But our public stance on gay marriage is not the only important factor to consider. We also want to take great care to preserve and deepen our friendships with gay friends, so that we have the continuing opportunity to share the love of Christ with them. So we must be careful to maintain a good witness on this issue, but that will also involve being equally careful about making sure they know how much their friendship is valued.

If *accepting* an invitation risks implying approval of gay marriage, *declining* one risks implying that their friendship is not important to us. So if we do need to decline a wedding invitation, we need to make sure we are investing in the friendship at the same time. That might mean extending an invitation to them; while not able to attend the wedding, nevertheless we should ask them round or out for an occasion as soon as we can.

Conclusion

I am the bread of life. Whoever comes to me will
never go hungry, and whoever believes in me will
never be thirsty.   *John 6 v 35*

Bread isn't something I tend to worry about. Within just a few hundred yards of my office there are
three supermarkets and well over a dozen sand-
wich shops. Bread is everywhere and I can't think of a
single occasion in my whole life when I needed some
but wasn't able to get hold of any.

In many parts of the world today this is not the case.
Nor was it so in the time of Jesus. Bread was *the* staple
food. This doesn't mean that everyone was unimagina-
tive and just decided to eat it every day. It means that
bread was the main thing they had to live on. Without
bread, people died. It wasn't a dull basic. It was a life es-
sential. No bread meant no life.

When we appreciate this, we can begin to get a sense
of what Jesus is claiming when he says: "I am the bread
of life." He is not an optional side that comes with

olives, oil and vinegar, to pick at before your "main" arrives. No, Jesus says he is the staple of life. He is what we need in order to truly live. Bread keeps our bodies going, but Jesus is what our souls need to live. Without him we are spiritual corpses.

Jesus being the bread of life is a concept I have been familiar with as a Christian for many years. I can't remember when I first came across it or first consciously thought about it. For as long as I've been a Christian, I've sort of always known it.

But it's a truth that has become especially dear to me as I have thought through the issue of same-sex attraction. Before, I'd always read it as just one of the things Jesus is. He's the light; he's the good shepherd; he's the way to the Father. And he's the bread of life. But more recently it has begun to hit home not so much that Jesus is *the bread of life*, but that *Jesus* is the bread of life. He—and he alone—is the one who satisfies.

One of the features of my own experience has been a tendency towards emotional over-dependency on particular friends. Over the years it has happened a number of times. Things with a good friend can be chugging along quite normally and quite happily, and then—almost out of the blue—I can feel a deep tug towards them: a profound need to be around them, to know their approval and affection. Left unchecked, this would quickly grow and grow. And before I know it, this person has become very close to being the center of my life. It's what the Bible calls idolatry, and it is unbearable. It creates deep yearnings that cannot be fulfilled, and it can put a terrible burden on the friendship.

And so it is a huge comfort to reflect on these words of Jesus. I can tell myself, on his authority, that he—and no other person, no other friend—is the bread of life. And he is. The more I live on that basis, the more true I know it to be. I can test him on it and know that he will always prove it. Life is far, far better when he is at the center, and far, far worse when anyone or anything else is.

This is, ultimately, the promise of the gospel. The great gift Jesus gives us is himself. He is not the means to some other end. It is not that the bread of life is something else, and Jesus happens to be the one who dispenses it. He himself is this bread. It is Jesus who satisfies our deepest emotional and spiritual needs. He is the prize—for all of us, irrespective of our issues and complexities. Anyone who comes to him will find fullness of life.

The invitation is there for everyone. And so precious is this gift that God cannot be truly said to be "anti" anyone to whom this wonderful gift is being offered.

What should I do if a Christian comes out to me?

Many Christians find it hard to talk openly to others about their struggles with SSA. If they are still coming to terms with it, there may be the fear that talking about it will somehow make it more real, as though the very act of speaking of it gives it a greater presence and significance.

There is also often a fear of how other Christians might respond: that friends will feel uncomfortable and might distance themselves; that church leaders will think anyone experiencing such feelings and temptations must be a great disappointment; or that admitting such things will only be letting the side down. The battle can feel lonely enough; the prospect that others might reject you if they knew can be enough to keep many Christians silent about their struggles for many long years.

This is all by way of saying that perhaps the first thing to do if a Christian ever discloses personal struggles with sexuality is **to thank them**. It will almost certainly have been a big deal for them to have shared this with you. They may have been psyching themselves up for months, getting to the point of raising it only to bottle it and put it off. That they have come this far and finally spoken of it—and done so to you—is no small thing. You may be the first or one of only a handful of people to have been told this. Any time someone shares something deeply personal, it is a sign of enormous trust. Acknowledge that. Thank them.

Let them take a few deep breaths and assure them

that the world is still spinning, that you're still there, and that they're not about to burst into flames.

The next thing to do is to **listen**—carefully. Experiences with SSA vary enormously. Points of sensitivity, triggers for temptation or despair, the issues surrounding and feeding into the feelings of attraction can differ enormously from one person to the next.

If they're happy to talk, find out how they are. Ask them how long they've known; what it's been like; what moved them to tell you. This may take some time. But it will help you get a sense of where they are with the issue, how it affects them and how they are responding to it as a Christian. Sometimes the experiences of SSA are just the symptoms of deeper issues of idolatry or insecurity. Sometimes there is family unhappiness in the background. Other times there is no obvious rhyme or reason to the feelings at all.

Gentle probing and careful listening will help to shape what sort of wisdom and counsel they may need. The Christian actively wrestling with these feelings, striving to flee from temptation, wanting to honor Christ and walk faithfully with him—they'll need encouragement, prayers and people to talk to from time to time.

Others may not be clear on the Bible's teaching on sex and sexuality, and will need some gentle instruction. Some may be in the depths of despair, imagining the presence of these feelings puts them spiritually beyond help, or feeling overwhelmed with guilt from past sins in this area. It may well be that they need some mentoring and help from a more experienced Christian or specialized ministry.

I f you are looking for further help with the issues raised in this book, the *Living Out* website is a great place to go. If you're **somebody who experiences same-sex attraction**, you will hear stories from a wide range of people who show that it's possible to stay loyal to what the Bible says and to flourish in life.

It's for you if you are **a church leader or member**—it aims to equip you to understand and care for the people in your church family who experience same-sex attraction.

And it's for t**he wider world** to listen in and find out that there is a different story. Many people think the church is homophobic, and that the church doesn't understand homosexuality. But the church isn't homophobic. The church does understand homosexuality and we want to be part of getting that message out to the world around us.

www.livingout.org

Why did Jesus have to die?

by Sam Allberry

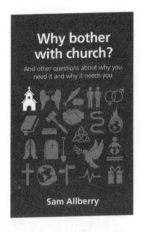

The church has an image problem. It is widely viewed as being outdated, boring, irrelevant and filled with backbiting hypocrites. How different that picture is to how the Bible talks about the new family that Jesus has gathered. It is a precious bride, a sparkling jewel, a lifeboat for forgiven sinners that is precious and holy; nurturing and warm; filled with truth, friendship and all embracing, forgiving love. This short, readable book explains clearly and simply what the church is and why it really matters.

A great series and an excellent resource. Important issues tackled thoughtfully, carefully, thoroughly and biblically. You couldn't ask for anything more. So don't. Buy these books and use them well.

Steve Timmis, Director Acts 29 Europe

thegoodbook.co.uk | thegoodbook.com
thegoodbook.com.au | thegoodbook.co.nz

Questions
Christians ask

Is forgiveness really free?

by Michael Jensen

Many Christians are confused by the relationship between the grace of God, and the role of laws and commands in the Christian life. What does it mean to live a life of grace? How does grace help us grow? And are we "once saved, always saved?" This short, readable book explores the Bible's teaching on these important questions and delivers some surprising and liberating conclusions.

> This great little book will warm your heart and stretch your mind. Rediscover why grace is so central not just in becoming a Christian but also in every day discipleship.

Krish Kandiah, Evangelical Alliance

thegoodbook.co.uk | thegoodbook.com
thegoodbook.com.au | thegoodbook.co.nz

uestions
Christians ask

Did the devil make me do it?
by Mike McKinley

When Jesus walked the earth, he cast out demons and had powerful encounters with the devil. But who exactly is the devil, and where did he come from? And what is he up to in the world today? This short, readable book explains clearly and simply what we can say with certainty from the Bible about Satan, demons and evil spirits.

Did the devil make me do it?

And other questions about Satan, demons and evil spirits

Mike McKinley

In his great little book, Mike McKinley tells us that the devil is real, ugly, dangerous and defeated. I've got lots of extra copies to use with others!

Mark Dever, Senior Pastor, Capitol Hill Baptist Church

thegoodbook
COMPANY

thegoodbook
COMPANY

BIBLICAL | RELEVANT | ACCESSIBLE

Thanks for reading this book. We hope you enjoyed it, and found it helpful.

Most people want to find answers to the big questions of life: Who are we? Why are we here? How should we live? But for many valid reasons we are often unable to find the time or the right space to think positively and carefully about them.

Perhaps you have questions that you need an answer for. Perhaps you have met Christians who have seemed unsympathetic or incomprehensible. Or maybe you are someone who has grown up believing, but need help to make things a little clearer.

At The Good Book Company, we're passionate about producing materials that help people of all ages and stages understand the heart of the Christian message, which is found in the pages of the Bible.

Whoever you are, and wherever you are at when it comes to these big questions, we hope we can help. As a publisher we want to help you look at the good book that is the Bible because we're convinced that as we meet the person who stands at its centre—Jesus Christ—we find the clearest answers to our biggest questions.

Visit our website to discover the range of books, videos and other resources we produce, or visit our partner site www.christianityexplored. org for a clear explanation of who Jesus is and why he came.

Thanks again for reading,

Your friends at The Good Book Company

UK & EUROPE
NORTH AMERICA
AUSTRALIA
NEW ZEALAND

thegoodbook.co.uk
thegoodbook.com
thegoodbook.com.au
thegoodbook.co.nz

0333 123 0880
866 244 2165
(02) 9564 3555
(+64) 3 343 2463

WWW.CHRISTIANITYEXPLORED.ORG
Our partner site is a great place for those exploring the Christian faith, with a clear explanation of the good news, powerful testimonies and answers to difficult questions.